THE WEIL LECTURES ON AMERICAN CITIZENSHIP

SOME CYCLES OF CATHAY

SOME CYCLES OF CATHAY

BY

WILLIAM ALLEN WHITE

AUTHOR OF
IN OUR TOWN; POLITICS: THE CITIZEN'S BUSINESS;
WOODROW WILSON; ETC.

CHAPEL HILL
THE UNIVERSITY OF NORTH CAROLINA PRESS
LONDON: HUMPHREY MILFORD
OXFORD UNIVERSITY PRESS
1925

Copyright, 1925, By
THE UNIVERSITY OF NORTH CAROLINA PRESS

THE PRESSES OF
THE SEEMAN PRINTERY INCORPORATED
DURHAM, N. C.

PREFACE

This book consists of a series of lectures delivered in the month of April, 1925, at the University of North Carolina under the auspices of the Weil Foundation, an unendowed lectureship on American Citizenship established by the University during the years 1914-1915. This is the ninth series since the initial lectures by ex-President William Howard Taft on "The Presidency: Powers, Duties, Obligations, and Responsibilities." Since that time the foundation, functioning through the Weil Lectures on American Citizenship, has been permanently established through the generosity of the families of Mr. Sol Weil and Mr. Henry Weil, of Goldsboro, North Carolina.

The lectures have been elaborated somewhat and probably have not been improved. In writing for an academic audience, so many restrictions and qualifications occur to a layman that he has probably cluttered the matter up hopelessly. Yet the thesis of the book, when it is finally set forth, is fairly simple: that our country has passed through three major political cycles, The Revolutionary Cycle, The Anti-Slavery Cycle, and The Populist Cycle; each cycle more or less duplicating the other and somewhat growing out of the other, and all three cycles being a part of a larger cycle of democratic growth in the peoples and governments controlled by the English speaking races. The thesis also would demonstrate that even those larger tribal cycles are a part of a still greater cycle of development known rather loosely as Christian civilization.

No historical thesis can be definitely proven. Such theses are interesting only as experiments in historical methods. Any theory which attempts to set forth definitely and finally an exact path of historical growth is subject to criticism and successful attack because the truth is too large for any theory; too elaborate to fit any thesis. But if this thesis, that our country has progressed in three cycles related to the growth of civilization under the influences of the Christian philosophy, attracts anyone, holds his interest and gives him a basis for further speculation, the purpose of the book is achieved. An author is not wise who would make men think as he thinks. He will be wise if he is content to make them think at all, to consider

"Whatsoever things are true, whatsoever things are honest, whatsoever things are just, . . . whatsoever things are of good report: if there be any virtue, and if there be any praise, think on these things."

—W. A. W.

EMPORIA, KANSAS.

CONTENTS

	PAGE
I. ARE HUMAN MOVEMENTS INDEPENDENT OF WARS?	1
II. THE LARGER CYCLE	15
III. THE EARLIER AMERICAN CYCLES	31
IV. THE LATER AMERICAN CYCLE	65
V. WHAT OF THE FUTURE?	91

SOME CYCLES OF CATHAY

*"Better Fifty Years of Europe
Than A Cycle of Cathay"*
—Locksley Hall

ARE HUMAN MOVEMENTS
INDEPENDENT OF WARS?

CHAPTER I

ARE HUMAN MOVEMENTS INDEPENDENT OF WARS?

In the nineteenth century it was fashionable for men to write books about battles—"great battles," they were supposed to be. Some one produced a ponderous tome detailing the movements of what were supposed to be the "Fifteen Decisive Battles of the World." To know history one was supposed to know the military or naval strategy of various titanic combats of men. The youth of fifty years ago who could not describe the tactics of Thermopolæ, who did not know about Blenheim, Malplaquet, and Ramillies, or who could not tell how the battle of Waterloo was won, was accounted neither a scholar nor a gentleman. How American youth pored over the manoeuvers of the generals at Yorktown, at New Orleans, at Gettysburg! Yet to-day few students think of going into the battles of the World War for important historical information. Perhaps this is because thinking people are about to conclude that none of these World War battles was in itself decisive. Perhaps even they are wondering if so far the results of the World War are not rather unimportant; are asking if, indeed, anything decisive came out of it!

Of course it is not true that war settles nothing. But it may be true that war settles nothing which the trend of human thinking and feeling would not have settled without war. Gettysburg turned back the forces of the Confederacy. But slavery would have been abolished if the Confederacy had won, and the disunion of a Confederate victory would surely have been short-lived. Yorktown overwhelmed Cornwallis, but one way or another a vigorous, restless, homogeneous, English-speaking colonial group such as ours was in 1776, settled chiefly by rebels and protestants of one sort or another, was sure to achieve independence one way or another—indeed was rapidly achieving independence before the Revolutionary War and could not have been checked in its political and economic development on this rich continent even if Yorktown had been won by Cornwallis. Waterloo settled precious little in Europe. Democracy rose in spite of the Holy Alliance, and the power of kings waned under the victory of the Allies. Historians are teaching the story of human progress with more and more emphasis upon the social and economic development of men and with smaller and smaller attention to the battles men fought. Except to teach youth how to fight other wars, it is folly to ask youth to consider the movements of troops and the tactics of generals upon any battlefield. Such military knowledge has just as much bearing upon the story of human progress as consideration of the chess games of the kings.

We are beginning to realize more and more that we may study human progress intelligently in just the proportion that we leave wars alone and confine our inquiries to what may be called the movements of mankind. War is comparatively easy to study. Movements are elusive. Yet they must have some sort of life-history; some more or less regular process of birth, growth, climax, and decay. Intelligent study of history seems to demand a new terminology for the course of what may be called the development of ideals. Movements are only aspirations dramatized. But what is their orderly process of drama? How shall we describe the drama's evolving stages? What shall we call the toxins and anti-toxins of the movements of humanity; the protagonists of an idea, and its opponents? Considering modern history biologically, we may say that Martin Luther was one kind of a bug or bacterium or bacillus and that he attacked certain other organisms in the blood of society and produced—Heaven only knows what; for the conflict is not finished. Modern civilization is still boiling with the Lutheran fever. And very likely it may be demonstrated that it was not the Luther bug at all that started the disturbance, but the Galilean bacillus or the Copernican germ. To isolate the spiritual first-cause of human epochs, to get him on a slide and consider him scientifically, is a vastly more important contribution to the knowledge of the world than to poke one's nose into old maps or to study the old scars on the body of man where the old boils of old wars once raged. The biological historian, considering ideas as living organisms that make movements, and tracing the life history of these movements, has an accurate and fascinating task.

In the chapters that follow, we shall attempt to look at three movements in American history, three cycles in our progress—if it is progress—not merely as the causes of our wars, but as periods in our development. It is likely that future historians considering a movement will find that a given change in the institutions of men comes through regular phases of development—not unlike a fever. The pathological story of political or economic change will be most interesting, and also perhaps helpful. From charts we may foretell events. Historians will hold prophets' licenses! We may develop a curve something like this: First the propagation of the original idea or thought plasm by some cloistered philosopher in academic shades, a vague formless mingling of syllogism with yearning. This low order of spiritual life will be exposed to the chill atmosphere of the social serenities—the ruling classes—and, apparently, will produce no infection. But ideas are highly infectious. They get into books and go to queer places. They endure all sorts of hardships, heat and cold, humidity and aridity. Often they survive without regeneration for a century, sometimes longer. Then here and there at isolated places emotional men—generally unthoughtful men, occasionally grossly ignorant and not altogether honest men,—are found exhibiting queer symptoms of mental dislocation. They are grumbling at the existing order, in some of its high and honorable points. Naturally and easily in the course of things these rattle-brains are dispersed. Others come to fill their places—many others, but not much more respectable than those who first appeared attacking Sacred Things. The political or social or economic infection, whatever it may be, then becomes recognized, definitely catalogued, named—probably in deep contumely. The classes whose privileges are threatened by the loose talk of irresponsible agitators quarantine against the distemper; editors, preachers, teachers, politicians, temple pharisees of various sorts, hurry out and spray venom against the dread disorder. They check it. The infection seems to have run its course.

Then it appears again in a new quarter, often under a new name—but the same old bug, hatched by the philosopher in his study. In its second appearance the virus seems strong. It attacks persons of social vitality. It often attaches itself to a political party. It becomes a raging epidemic, and in that stage gets back into the colleges from which it started. Some strong man appears, with a berserker rage, clear gone with the poison of the bug.

Then—behold the agitator, the man with a cause! Like a moth to a flame he circles nearer and nearer to his end, generally to his ruin and death. But the protagonist infects the multitude, and the new idea, scarcely recognizable as the mild philosophic precept of the pantalooned and slippered philosopher by his hearth, scourges the land, taking a social or political form or an economic statement, and so comes the revolution.

Strong, calm men in a fine, firm manner take charge of the idea, administer it in a war or in a bloodless revolution, and then, at the end of the epidemic, when the incendiary idea has infected and so immunized the population, when the people no longer resist the innovation in considerable masses,—these strong, calm, firm men walk over to the parks and climb on pedestals, and turn into statues erected by a grateful and infected people.

Some such historic curve as this will be worked out when historians quit piddling with battles and turn to the isolation of the bacilli that make the battles. For, to continue the figure, if the social germ has in it the vitality of truth, it will persist in defeat, after battles, through wars, and in spite of treaties that would destroy it. Proclamations of kings and potentates cannot destroy the truth, even though the proclamations have behind them all the soldiers in all the armies in all the world. No high explosive is so powerful as the repression of truth.

From these polemics let us get back to earth. Our American history, even though nearly three hundred years old, is comparatively contemporary. Its sources are fairly authentic. Its documents permit little controversy. If they have revealed little to support a modern view of historical criticism, possibly they have not been read in the light of modern historical methods. But there they are—the full records of a people's development, from a pioneer people to a world-leading nation. When the data is examined by the economist, by the psychologist, by the diagnosing physician, by the biologist who can trace strains of heredity, by the sociologist who can understand and interpret causes of social unrest, we shall then have a history written that will explain our past; a history indeed that will explain our present. How inevitable it is! How inexorably it has grown out of our past!

Things don't just happen in this world. America was no accident. The change of no one event, the reversal of no ten or a dozen chances upon which events seemed to hinge would have made great difference in our destiny. Individuals have counted little. If any one had failed, another likely might have appeared. Times may make men, perhaps more than men affect their times. The divinely appointed agent probably after all is only an agent. Another might have been commissioned if the first one failed. Europe and America had reached about the same evolutionary status before the World War, with quite a different set of leaders, and in a rather different path of progress. The ideas back of the two civilizations were essentially the same. The results were to be the same. The seeding and the harvest of these ideas is our common progress. If we breed a certain type of mind in man, give him by heredity a certain emotional content, a certain strength of will, his civilization will be the reflex of his endowments. One of the nice problems for future historians to solve is to determine which is the cart and which the horse in drawing civilizations to their attainments: whether ideas affect humanity, or whether humanity bred to a certain racial norm accepts, gestates, and gives birth to the political progeny of certain ideals. For instance—was it the Christian ideals which produced the complex social organism that we call Western Civilization? Or did the Caucasian race develop Christianity and its democratic implications? Again—did the English Bill of Rights produce Jefferson and so the Declaration of Independence, and our peculiar loathing of kings and love of plutocrats; or did the British breed, environed by a new continent, teeming with economic opportunity, produce a race here that had no time to salute kings while it was chasing economic opportunities? It is all very puzzling. But whatever answer one makes, he cannot escape the inevitableness of destiny. Call the impulsion of destiny what you will, the orderly working of laws or the order that decreed the laws, purpose is there—a greater purpose than human purpose. That purpose holds the stars in their courses; why protest if we call it Divine purpose?

Then again, why should we fear to find that the God of Battles is a minor god? Why rage if we maintain that the favor of the God of Battles buys nothing for the race? He helps generals and kings, and sometimes politicians, but the people in their deep purposes are not stopped by the outcome of wars. When we go further into the examination of the three larger cycles of American history, we shall find, perhaps, that these larger cycles of our history are a part of a still larger cycle in world history; that the philosophical ideas which fired our blood as Americans were derived from older and greater ideas; and that our three cycles are curves in some great march of humanity going—God only knows where!

THE LARGER CYCLE

CHAPTER II

THE LARGER CYCLE

The story of man's occupation of the earth seems to be divided into two rather sharply marked periods—the ancient and the modern world. It is not altogether a distinction of time; somewhat it is of space. For more than half of mankind is living in the ancient world to-day for all practical purposes. We of Europe and the Western Hemisphere and of certain islands of the Western seas are proud of our modernity. Perhaps our pride is based too heavily upon the modern machinery that we use so universally. We are prone to forget that it is the universality of the use of machinery and not the mere use of machinery which differentiates us from our brothers of a darker skin. And we use machinery so generally in our modern civilization, diffuse its benefits so widely, share its profits somewhat equitably among all those whose work goes into our modern civilization, chiefly because we of the Western world are impregnated with an idea

—the idea of democracy, which is, speaking broadly, Christianity rather roughly institutionalized. Our keenest minds are inventors of machines because invention pays. Invention pays because we have so wide a market for machines. And our market is wide because we have so ordered our industry, our commerce, our institutions of government that the average man is a potential user and beneficiary of every profitable invention that comes from the brain of his fellows. We are fairly well levelled so that white men are standardized in their living. Which is to say, we are brethren, not master and man; and that relation implies the acceptance of the Golden Rule of the philosophy of Christianity.

The difference between the ancient world and the modern world, wherever those worlds may exist in time or space, is the difference of ideals upon which the two worlds are founded. The ancient world seems to have risen upon the theory that physical force is man's final arbiter. The modern world seems to be growing upon the faith that ideas rule; that things of the spirit are unconquerable when they promote broader fellowships, more abundant living, more kindly grace in the works and ways of men.

THE LARGER CYCLE 17

These two worlds, the ancient and the modern world, so deeply different, in so far as they are separated by time, have their records of beginning and growth. We find these records imbedded in the most permanent form they could have taken—in the story of our Western religion. It is curious to find that the story of the beginnings of the ancient world and the story of the beginnings of the modern world are written in our Bible. To me at least it is immaterial whether these stories of beginnings, the story in Genesis, and the story in the Gospels of the New Testament, are actual records or symbolic myths. It seems quite as miraculous that the prophetic mind of man could divine the tremendous truths of the story of the seven days of creation as in Genesis or could have proclaimed the basic philosophy of a democratic civilization as in the Gospels and could set them forth symbolically and scientifically true, as it is miraculous that the Creator and Savior of humanity should have done the marvels which the Scriptures declare were done, and then inspired the heart of the man who set down these mighty epics.

So, without raising the question whether the story be symbolic fable or authentic history, let us examine the beginnings of this modern world. We find it most strikingly set forth in the story accredited in the New Testament to the writer Luke. To the writers of the other Gospels we must go for environing details. The story that Luke tells us is of two women of Nazareth: an old woman named Elizabeth "well stricken in years," the wife of a certain Zacharias, who "in the order of his course," among other things, executed the priest's office. The other woman was her younger and comelier cousin, Mary, the wife of a village carpenter. They sat in the stone hut where the elder woman dwelt and of course the two were talking of their babies about to be born. They were poor, decent folk, these two expectant mothers, who lived in an oppressed land. Files of Roman soldiers passed upon the high road through their province going out to conquer the farther East. Plunder, rapine, murder, all the offenses of an invading army upon a defenseless and subject people these women saw, and their hearts were bitter. As motherhood came upon them with its solemnities, these women going about their daily work, yearning for a deliverer for their stricken land, voiced the anguish of their hearts. And the story says that Mary, the younger, being newly wed, and of the lyric age, made a song. And a wonderful song it is, that song of the daughter of the tribe of Aaron there in that little stone hut upon the hillside of Nazareth. Cried the exultant Mary:

> My soul doth magnify the Lord,
> And my spirit hath rejoiced in God my saviour.
> For he hath regarded the low estate of his handmaiden. . . .
> For he that is mighty hath done to me great things. . . .
> He hath showed strength with his arm;
> He hath scattered the proud in the imagination of their hearts.
> He hath put down the mighty from their seats,
> And exalted them of low degree.
> He hath filled the hungry with good things,
> And the rich he hath sent empty away.
> He hath holpen his servant Israel in remembrance of his mercy.

"And Mary," continues the narrative, "abode with her (cousin) about three months and returned to her house."

And so with the aspirations of those two women of Israel, daughters of the tribe of Aaron, the older woman carrying the child of her "stricken years," Mary in the joy of youth and love eagerly awaiting the fulfillment of her dream, there in the land of a shamed and captive people, where the brilliant cruel pageant of the old world at the apex of its glory filed by their doors, burning upon their hearts the emblems of its power, there sat these two seers of a great hope that was to be a new order. And there with that pathetic exaltation of Mary the modern world began.

This is declaring in poetical terms a fact which may be stated scientifically: That as man began to organize his life under law, instead of under the whim of his despots, he began to dignify his individual humanity, and as a corollary of the dignity which he was assuming, all men, even the most lowly, found in their hearts some aspiration toward justice. This aspiration began to make history with the opening centuries of the Christian era.

A new dynamic idea was born in the world when the common man felt and declared his rights. The death of Jesus of Nazareth on Calvary Hill dramatized the idea of the rights of man, although it laid weight upon the duties of man. But when men are taught by the Golden Rule to treat others as equals, they naturally demand that others treat them as equals, and this demand for dignity of the individual human spirit slowly forced its way into the institutions of Europe.

The history of Europe from the time of Cæsar Augustus, who decreed "that all the world should be taxed," for nearly two thousand years has been the story of the struggle of man's spirit to attain its dignity. The struggle was first manifested in the realm of religion. For the state was too powerfully entrenched in force—the force of tradition, the force of arms, the force of property rights to be at first affected by the altruistic ideals of the Nazarene Carpenter. So His doctrine of the essential dignity of man's spirit gathered to itself a dogma, a plan of salvation, a religious organization, many rituals, an elaborate system of taboos enforced by a hierarchy. This hierarchy finally overthrew the state. But the dogma, the plan of salvation, the taboos, all were levellers—all taught men that they were equal in spirit, equal in their obligations to God and man, equal in the next world by reason of duties done in this. Thus behind the shield of the Holy Church and its faith came the unconquerable aegis of the Golden Rule and the Beatitudes. And back of them by inexorable implication they brought democracy into the world.

The Holy Faith overshadowed the state. But democracy after the Reformation overthrew the temporal power of the Holy Faith. So with many cross-currents, with eddies that came from the externals of passing times and led nowhere, and in spite of obstructions that fell before it, the stream of human progress in that part of mankind known as the Western world flowed swiftly toward the civilization that we know to-day and are pleased to call a Christian civilization; not, alas, for what it has attained, but for what it should attain.

For it is a gay, hard civilization, this Western civilization; a machine-rattling, God-mocking civilization, that is just now going through a phase which is dangerous only if it is prolonged, a phase of cynical reaction against a vain and wicked war, and a futile punitive peace.

To many who have bound up their lives in the faith of an order that is passing this change of to-day seems decay. We need a larger faith that we may see the substance of things hoped for in the sad evidence of things not seen. The test of a man's faith comes not when he is fighting, but after he has won. To see that reaction is a mere pause of the current of life, gathering strength for some new impulse toward unvisioned nobilities; to stand by and see unafraid one's ideals, like Shadrach, Meshach, and Abednego, all pass into the fiery furnace of realization, that is the mountain-moving faith. So, saluting unflinchingly all that is passing before us, let us be of stout heart; for to-morrow we shall smile at to-day's fears. What if in every field of human endeavor we see evidences that man is trying to close his heart to the appeal of brotherhood! Politics is highly divisory; shattered with factions, blocs, klans, and Heaven knows what of small exclusive organisms—but what then! Religion is threatened with intolerant schisms—all right, it is the way of the human heart before it begets its new ideals. Business is rejecting state regulation and taking Cain's attitude toward the public. Well—so be it. Pride goeth before destruction! In literature leadership is falling into the hands of a cult that is clearly on the side of the devil's own angels, the side that scoffs at any theory that there is a moral purpose guiding our destiny. Art is full of ugliness, disharmonies, barbaric yawps crying out against the canons of beauty as the devils of sentimentality. All that we once aspired to be seems to be forgotten and only the baseness in what we are is exalted. Still let us be of good cheer. The world did not end with Sodom. Hard times are these, springing out of hard hearts. They tell us who man the watch towers that the reaction which is sweeping over Western civilization is bringing America, which for three centuries has been developing its own ideals, its own expressions of democracy, into alarming conformity to the European norm; that our morals are becoming Europeanized; that our politics is growing shamelessly cynical. In fear the tribunes of liberty cry out that property rights never flaunted themselves more brazenly under Augustus Cæsar than they hail themselves masters of human destiny in America to-day. But we must have faith to know that indeed does the Lord guard the city and that the watchers do not watch in vain.

To renew our faith it may be well to go back to another day—a day in America when we were working out our own civilization—a mean thing perhaps, but our own—in our own way, after the visions in our own hearts. For surely in the swift progress of America during 300 years we may find so straight and clear a path that reviewing it one may bolster his belief in some purposeful guidance of humanity toward a more abundant life. Surely the expansion of opportunity to live freely, justly, happily, usefully, and in consequent self-respect, has been so steady and so wide in the three centuries of our occupation of this continent that we may well accept, with certain sophisticated restrictions and a few amiable qualifications, much of the gaudy dream of our fathers of the "manifest destiny" of our country. Therefore it may be wise to recall that earlier day; to consider American civilization as it once worked itself out, not of course independently of Europe, but synchronously, differing in degree somewhat, as our background of heredity and environment differs from the European background.

The purpose of these pages shall be to withdraw from the consideration of the onward sweep of progress as it affected our European cousins during the last two or three centuries and to take thought of our own peculiar problems, as they have developed. Thus taking thought of ourselves as Americans we may revive the hope that despite the machines which are huddling humanity together upon the planet there may be some peculiar use for America as America in the scheme of things, closely interrelated with the world, a part of the world, but still ourselves.

So admitting, of course, that we are new, that we are of necessity crude, that we have the savage faults of our strength, bringing here no faint denial that fifty years of Europe are better than a cycle of Cathay,—let us review three of those cycles. The surface of humanity has changed, but the heart of man is changeless. Maybe there is in a study of these formative years of our Republic something to be learned that will help us understand our land, and even the world that is to be.

We may find here in this story of our own growth something that will help us to understand the ways of human development. We may even see in our cycles of Cathay, in the two or three hundred years of our journey into the wilderness of this continent, some epitome of the evolution of the democratic ideal—some typical life history of the spiritual plasm of our era that will help us to know our destiny, to recognize our way in the world, to follow the light that God has given us.

Of course, in casting our history into these cycles one has to be arbitrary. There are restrictions and qualifications in any statement of historical theory. But these three periods of our history do seem to have a common spiritual impulse and if linked may explain the story of America's rise and growth. Possibly the spiritual impulse back of us may even forecast our destiny.

THE EARLIER AMERICAN CYCLES

CHAPTER III

THE EARLIER AMERICAN CYCLES

When the British colonies were settled in the seventeenth and eighteenth centuries, a new top was set spinning in the world. It was not different from the English top, especially at first, but it came to have a different speed and a slightly different direction as the centuries passed. The difference between human development in Great Britain and in the English-speaking colonies of the North American hemisphere was due somewhat to a new and different environment which produced new and different social and economic conditions. But also heredity had much to do with the change. During the seventeenth century and possibly the earlier part of the eighteenth century, one hundred thousand British subjects came to the Colonies. They were, for the most part, adventurers of one sort or another—a lot that did not believe in the conventions of the time; the social conventions, the religious conventions, the political conventions. Probably England was glad to be rid of them. They were disturbers of traffic. By 1776 that hundred thousand had increased to more than a million and a half, chiefly by breeding, and they inbred their kind —adventurers, malcontents, nonconformists, protestants against the established order. The Colonists differed from the inhabitants of Great Britain because they were troublemakers and adventurers—selectively bred. They went out from England because they were cramped in one way or another, or adventure-hungry. Then the soil of the eastern seaboard of the continent in which the Colonists settled was not in general as rich as that of England. In the valleys only was the cultivated soil good enough to sustain a profitable agriculture. So it happened that in New England and the middle states traders predominated. Traders and professional men made the public sentiment. The towns led the country. The opinions of Boston, New York, and Philadelphia were the governing opinions. In the South leadership of public opinion rested outside of the yeomen. The Atlantic ocean sawed out a score of harbors on the North American coast and these harbors made merchants even of the southern planters. They, with their slaves, became in effect manufacturers and merchants. They were exporting cotton, rice, and cane products and bringing in more or less food and much lovely and exotic merchandise needed to maintain a luxurious plantation civilization. Thus the planters became the aristocracy of the port towns. These traders north and south, who were born and bred in rebellion against the commercial restrictions of the mother country, were unrestrained in their revolutionary designs by a local hereditary-aristocracy—authentic and of royal blood and patronage. The nobility and gentry of the colonies, excepting officialdom, were mostly home made—the merchants, planters, lawyers of the countryside raised to some not very mysterious "n"th power. So the local nobility, even when it was Tory, had small restraining influence. And often it was not Tory and at times was incendiary. Not infrequently in the quarter century before the Revolution did these local squires sit back and publicly disapprove of mob violence inspired in a rabble incited by the bitter complaints of the stable classes of society. All this was unlike England of that period. The British top was spinning perhaps as fast, but in another orbit. This difference in course made separation of the two countries—England and the British Colonies—inevitable.

The Colonists, expanding since 1776, with what influx immigration we have gained in 150 years, number over one hundred million people in the United States; a different civilization from that of the mother country, differing perhaps not so much in kind as in degree—but certainly different. Yet our history is more like British history than like French or German or Russian history. Our political, social, and religious movements, particularly the earlier movements, have been extensions of somewhat similar movements in the mother country. Roughly speaking, we have had, in this extension of our history, in this different phase of revolutionary change, three epochs, the three cycles of Cathay, if you will, rather distinct, yet each coming out of its predecessor as a natural evolutionary consequence of environment and heredity. The three epochs are all a part of the history of those who in England and the other English-speaking colonies are of the English race and blood.

Our first cycle of change may well be called the American Revolution, yet it was so insolubly a part of the British development that the war should not have been called a revolutionary war but a civil war. Lexington and Yorktown were the internecine struggles of Englishmen, of Britons, as much as Bosworth Field and Marston Moor.

Our revolutionary struggle was the beginning of a change which separated our problems from those of Great Britain. So it must be considered, this American Revolution, as a part of a new order.

Following the Revolution came another movement in our politics which made a cycle in our history. It is known as the anti-slavery movement. And following that came the third cycle, which has not been historically named—perhaps the cycle has not even been historically completed. But, by way of identification, we may call it the Populist movement. Now these three cycles, our revolutionary movement of the eighteenth century, our anti-slavery movement of the nineteenth century, and our Populist movement which began in the latter half of the nineteenth century and has extended into the first quarter of this century, are beads strung upon a single string. That string is the philosophy of John Locke, a seventeenth century philosopher, who first in the English-speaking world proclaimed the natural rights of man. Locke held that human rights existed before the foundation of society; that government is a means devised by man for the better enjoyment of man's natural rights; that the state is made by man for man and not man for the state. This philosophy uttered in the seventeenth century was social dynamite. Of course, it is a political corollary of the philosophy of Jesus, the inevitable logical sequence which follows the theoretical acceptance of the Golden Rule as a political premise. And for 1700 years the Holy Church had been upholding in theory at least the doctrine of the Golden Rule; so it had impregnated the thinking of Christendom. It is fascinating to watch a philosophical precept entering practical human life, and like a force of nature blowing institutions to bits, leading men to their death, changing maps, and diverting racial destinies. Of course the mere publication of an idea produces small immediate effect: perhaps only the crucifixion or the exile of the thinker; perhaps mere social ostracism; perhaps not even that, perhaps only a certain forehead tapping among the philosopher's most intimate enemies. It is when an idea dominates the will of some strong man and when he consecrates his life to that idea that it becomes the Archimedean lever that moves the world.

John Locke had been dead and in his grave nearly three quarters of a century before his idea began to ferment in the American colonies and produce a nation. Not until Sam Adams, "the chief incendiary" of the American Revolution, began to dramatize in politics—very practical politics, often, probably, corrupt politics —the political theories of Locke, did those theories, having fallen on good ground, begin to ripen for the harvest.

It is odd when we consider American history, indeed all history, to note what humble instruments fate uses to produce great changes in life. Sam Adams, to whose agitation against the British Parliament we owe probably more than to any other one man our identity as an American nation, by our modern definitions would be called a crank. He had failed as a business man, failed as an office holder in not having collected his quota as a tax collector, and he failed even to provide properly for his family. Probably his failure in his twenties, thirties, and early forties furnished the goad for him through some devilish inferiority complex which spurred him on when he found that he could achieve results in politics. He was obsessed by a hatred of Great Britain. His father's fortune had been overturned by an act of Parliament which dissolved a land bank wherein Sam Adams's father's fortune was lodged and invested. It must not be assumed that Adams was consciously seeking revenge upon Great Britain for the destruction of the land bank. Men are rarely motived consciously in their emotional activities. It is even as unfair to Adams to say that he was getting even with Parliament for wrecking the land bank as it is to say that the British Parliament deliberately set out to exploit and alienate the Colonies. The Parliament may seem like a cruel cat dealing with a helpless mouse in its American attitude of the eighteenth century; passing obnoxious legislation, then repealing it after it had been ignored or flaunted. But the cat and mouse figure is unjust; better is that of the hen and the duckling. The British government could not conceive of a people like the Americans. The British were making laws for a people which they thought were home-staying Englishmen. The new race that had been bred of the British adventurers in a wilderness was too much for Parliament to comprehend.

Sam Adams entered politics through the Boston town meeting by building up as effective and probably as unscrupulous a political machine as ever controlled a caucus, and dominated by minority insistence the course of a larger convention. But he was more than a machine politician. He also wrote and agitated for his cause. It is rare that a man has the capacity to control caucuses and wield a pen. But Adams did each well. During the fifty years before the Declaration of Independence there had been in America rising and falling tides of revolt against Great Britain—rising at every new legislative act of Parliament seeking to control the finances and commerce of the colonies and falling as the act was rescinded or abandoned. The government made mistakes; the people grumbled, sometimes even rioted. The governmental mistakes were often corrected and little by little most of the American colonies began to live in a semi-detached status from the mother country. Many of the colonies paid their own governors by taxes imposed by colonial legislature and the legislature withheld the gubernatorial salaries if the governors did not obey the representatives of the people. So it was easy to redress the wrong which England imposed. The people controlled the legislatures. This power of the legislatures gave the people the power to withhold salaries of the executive and judicial branches of their government. Many colonial charters gave to the people virtual control of the administrative as well as the legislative branches of the government, so that during those fifty ante-revolutionary years the colonies gradually were assuming an independence of the British government not unlike the independence which the English-speaking democracies of other lands have gained through gradual changes as the centuries have gone by.

But Sam Adams came ten or a dozen years before the Declaration of Independence with his Boston caucus, with his grievance against the British Parliament, with his terrible talent for controversy and agitation. Year by year he injected a bitterness into the situation which kept wounds from healing. These unhealed wounds together with the accumulated blunders of the British Parliament produced in the hearts of the colonists a Cause. Sam Adams's talent for organization led him to intrigue with other colonies and so we had the inter-colonial revolt, the organized attack upon Great Britain. And what had become for more than a century a gradual and natural loosening of bonds became, under Adams and the patriots of the Continental Congress, a revolutionary cause, a cause having, of course, an economic basis but a political statement.

And it was the political statement rather than the economic basis which produced the revolution. It was not that the taxes imposed by Great Britain in the last ten years of the pre-revolutionary period were economically intolerable. These taxes were never paid. If they had been paid they would not have been destructive. But an idea had been planted in the hearts of a free people—"no taxation without representation"—an idea of oppression, an aspiration for sheer justice, an idea based upon the theory that man had natural rights, that the state was created for his prosperity and happiness, that interference with that prosperity and happiness on behalf of the state was an intolerable tyranny. The American Revolution was produced by that idea rather than by the actual economic injustices which were symbols of the violation of the American ideals. Of course Adams had his prototypes in other colonies. South Carolina, where Rutledge lived, had her tea party. Women conducted it. It was revolutionary and is celebrated to-day in Charleston. The struggle of all the colonies against what they came to deem British injustice and oppression is somewhat a typical struggle in each of the colonies. But Adams was one of the first inter-colonial figures in the pre-revolutionary struggle. For ten years in Boston Adams stood as the protagonist of the revolutionary cause; a man of one idea devoted so exclusively to politics that when he came into political success his neighbors refurbished him, gave him decent clothes, painted his barn, and endowed him with a fund with which to support his family. Through all his machinations against the British Parliament (and he was a practical ward boss, was Sam Adams, as well as a fervid agitator and an intrepid revolutionist) he had apparently no considerable means of support. It was natural that the Tories, men who worked for an honest living, who had some property interest in the land, who believed in law and order, and very likely called it "lawr and o'duh," who had no desire for revolution, who believed in equitable compromise, regarded this unkempt, frowsy, beggarly revolutionist with his tracts and his ward heelers as the incarnation of wicked, self-seeking, irresponsible anarchy.

To them he was a living firebrand spreading chaos in an orderly land. He emphasized every blunder of the British Parliament, every mistake of its representatives in the colonies, and used those blunders and mistakes to inflame the people. What he really was doing was inculcating into their hearts the dynamic doctrine of the natural rights of man—those dangerous theories of government which were predicated upon the Golden Rule and the Beatitudes. He did not know his original Biblical sources. He rarely mentioned them. But the philosophy of altruism restated in Locke's thesis that the state is built for its subjects and that no subject is bound to an unjust state, when converted into a political pabulum under the heat of human blunders in an absentee government, produced the Declaration of Independence.

Of course we must not fail to give credit to the other revolutionaries of the colonies. The Carolinas had their eloquent Rutledge; Virginia had Patrick Henry, also an orator, and Washington a smouldering firebrand, and Jefferson the scholar who took from Rousseau all that Sam Adams had from Locke. Also the indefatigable Franklin in Pennsylvania did his part as an agitator. He had little philosophy from books. Locke and Rousseau came to him translated freely into life, which he read voraciously. The agitators of the revolution were like all agitators—not the solid pillars of society. Washington, alone of the lot, was a man of great wealth—most of which he married. And while Sam Adams was rabble-rousing in the sixties, Washington was earning as honest a living as any Tory and having fellowship with Lord Fairfax.

The Declaration of Independence at Philadelphia came only after war had been raging nearly two years. It was clearly an afterthought of the war, as the Emancipation Proclamation was—a military necessity. It was preceded probably by outbursts of patriotic zeal like the Mecklenburg Declaration. But it was the work of the agitators nevertheless, the child of John Locke through Sam Adams, "the chief incendiary" of the revolution! Like all human documents, the Declaration of Independence is full of errors. Many of its conclusions are based upon an inaccurate statement of facts, a partisan presentation of events, which calm historical criticism must eradicate. But the Declaration, bursting upon civilization like a rocket in 1776, became a worldwide statement of the

Nazarene thesis in political terms. Upon the utterance of the Declaration, the revolution was finished. It needed only a few years of fighting to establish the creed in history as the spiritual embryo of a new national consciousness.

But alas, governments in that day could not rest any more than they do to-day upon "the consent of the governed." "The consent of the governed" is a pleasant fiction which the American people in their wrath at Great Britain invented as a battle slogan.

When the siege of Yorktown ceased, government, as an orderly process in which justice is compromised with expediency and the consent of the governed is obtained in many devious ways, had to begin to function. In those days and for two decades before the Revolution the Tories had rather a hard time. They were banged about and battered physically, spiritually, and financially rather severely. But later they regained their prestige. Those forces of society which work regularly, trade cannily, aspire temperately, and invest wisely must in the nature of things work out the problems which are presented after any great upheaval of the more radical forces of society. In these post-revolutionary days and in the decades that followed came the necessary period of reaction.

A certain amount of odium unjustly attaches to the term reaction in politics. The term signifies nothing more than a period of calm adjustment, through common use, of those laws, customs, and institutions that have been born out of impassioned visions. For nearly two hundred years before the Revolution, political theories of a rather advanced character had occupied the mind of not merely the visionaries but of a considerable minority of the people. Their detachment from the mother country, their peculiar heritage of protestantism in its purest essence, bred in many Americans—who had become a nation of merchants—a taste for all sorts of political freedom and independence. Many of the charters of the colonies hung by slight threads of rather unobserved tradition upon Parliamentary authority. In Boston, even the King's troops were subject to indirect orders from Sam Adams after the Boston massacre. The people for a century had withheld salaries from judges and governors and controlled them by a sort of direct democracy in many colonies. In the vision of the revolutionary, this order was presumed; they believed it would continue forever. In the period of reaction, while the constitution was forming and during its first decade of trial, Americans found that under stable government many of the visions of the pre-revolutionary patriots had to give way to the common sense of men like Hamilton, Washington, Madison, and Monroe. Hence, this first period of reaction settled many things; established many institutions; set our country in its course, quite a different course from that which the agitators of the fifties and sixties in the eighteenth century had dreamed their country would take. So came our Constitution.

Now the American Constitution judged pragmatically is the wisest political document written by man. It has worked. For nearly a century and a half it has bound together a nation that has grown from less than three millions to more than one hundred millions with only one manifestation of force. Ours is the oldest written charter on the globe that has survived the wrack and expansion of modern ideas under which all other written constitutions have crumbled. Our Constitution has gathered into it the political wisdom of two thousand years—saving every good thing. It is built upon the practical application in daily living of the Nazarene philosophy put into such concrete terms of compromise with reality as man's present physical breeding and spiritual inheritance require in his economic environment. It embodies in dogmatic checks and balances of rights and liberties all that the Declaration of Independence proclaimed as the ideal of human relations under government. Always there must be an interpreter—a transformer, if you will—to take the pure current of idealism and reduce it to practical creed. Paul followed Jesus. It had to be. The Constitution followed the Declaration. Washington followed Sam Adams and Jefferson. Lincoln followed Phillips and Garrison; as the constitutional amendments followed the Emancipation Proclamation, and as Roosevelt and Wilson followed Altgeld and Bryan.

Yet the force which adopted our American Constitution differed probably deeply in kind rather than in degree from the force which created the Revolution and wrote the Declaration. Each of these forces, mutually repellant, is a necessary force in life. Your conservatives and your liberals, your radicals and your reactionaries represent principles necessary to the healthy functioning of a body politic. And after our revolutionary fever had subsided, the slow, steady building up of the body, the recuperation of trade, the convalescence of order, the stabilizing of politics and business became the work of the more centripetal forces of life on the American continent. The functions of an absentee Parliament were resumed under the institutions erected by our Constitution. Sam Adams, the firebrand of the sixties, seventies, and eighties of the eighteenth century became, by the sheer force of years, a rather futile, half-ignored, more or less petted, gently tolerated political figure who faded out of the new pattern that was moving on the loom of life in his country. In this second century since he lived and wrought, Sam Adams has become only a name. School boys and historians, who stop to examine the sources of our Revolution, know Sam Adams as the father of the Revolution. But to most, he is only a waxwork figure. Washington, the Father of his Country, stands in the immortal bronze, a respectable man, hardly at all an agitator, never an incendiary, a successful military revolutionist but not a rabble-rousing rebel.

Our first cycle in America was not ended even with the adoption of the Constitution.

Our political independence from Great Britain was not achieved until the establishment of the Monroe Doctrine. And the stabilization of internal government was not completed until the adoption of the Bill of Rights. The victory which the men of the Sam Adams type achieved in 1776 at Independence Hall in Philadelphia was carried on by Jefferson who left powerful residuary legatees in our politics—men who for a century and a quarter have been giving powerful voice to the national aspiration for justice. But it may well be assumed that during the first and second decades of the nineteenth century the forces set in motion by the American Revolution of the eighteenth century were fairly well stabilized. That cycle was beginning to approach its close. How the old patriots of the sixties and seventies of the eighteenth century must have rejoiced in their work! For them, the world struggle for justice was finished. For them, the millennium had come. For them, progress was ended. For they, as a part of the curse which time puts into the blood of men, had become old, conservative, static.

How they must have looked askance at the new force of discontent abroad in the land!

THE EARLIER AMERICAN CYCLES 51

Indeed, Sam Adams came to view Shay's rebellion as the devil's own work. Yet it was a rebellion against taxes even as the Adams rebellion was in the seventeen sixties and early seventies. And in the first two decades of the nineteenth century, when there were grumblings among Americans from the same social and spiritual ranks as the revolutionists of the mid-eighteenth century, the conservative veterans of the Revolutionary War must have frowned upon the malcontents of their day. These malcontents were springing up not in the line of progress which the elder rebels had marked out but from a new area in our spiritual terrain. The new prophets of discontent were complaining at the injustices of slavery, at the political iniquities of what they called the slaveholding oligarchy of the South in the economic policies of the nation. The riots which the colonies saw in the forties, fifties, and sixties before the Revolution, the riots in which Tories were maltreated and their homes stoned, men began to see in the thirties, forties, and fifties of the next century after the Revolution. But in the early nineteenth century it was the conservative forces of society which mobbed the radicals. The Abolitionists became a pest in orderly government. In Boston, where the Tories had seen Sam Adams with his caucus control town meetings and order colonial troops from shore to ship, in Boston, where Tories had first inveighed against his assumptions of the functions of the government and then turned tail and fled to Salem, in Boston the orderly forces of society turned a hard and bitter heart toward the Abolitionists. Garrison was dragged through the streets; Wendell Phillips saw him. Benjamin Lundy had been a pioneering Abolitionist for a dozen years. He had been threatened, maligned, abused; his business destroyed; his person insulted; and his spirit traduced. For three decades, Lundy went up and down America making a Cause. He and Garrison and Phillips, too, proclaimed, though in a different vernacular, what Sam Adams and Otis proclaimed in Boston and Patrick Henry in Virginia and Rutledge in the Carolinas—the natural rights of man. But the Abolitionists appealed more consciously, more passionately, to the philosophy of Jesus. Garrison and Phillips took up the banner when Lundy laid it down in the little town of Lowell, Illinois. Of course, even as the basis of Adams's political protest against Great Britain pretended to be economic, so was this protest of Phillips and Garrison and the Abolitionists fundamentally and really economic. The moral issue which they presented and which Adams presented was only the restatement of an economic mal-adjustment in ethical terms, as Adams had stated in ethical terms a political mal-adjustment. As he clamored, a rabid agitator, for political independence, so the Abolitionists, equally rabid but not more unreasonable, clamored for the economic freedom of labor in terms of moral justice. The economic hypothesis of the slavery problem was something like this: that so long as men under compulsion worked for a mere living without self-respect, their competitors outside of slavery could have no self-respect because they could not earn more than a bare living wage in competition with slave labor. Of course that statement of the case rarely was made. The moral obliquity of slavery appealed to the emotions of the people more quickly and more forcefully than its economic unbalance. So the moral appeal aroused the popular wills to action more readily than the economic statement of the case. Indeed, so many moral issues in this world are really economic issues couched in emotional language!

Just as Sam Adams made the economic problems of the Boston merchants of the eighteenth century eventually seem to require political independence, so it was soon evident in the Abolitionist agitation of the nineteenth century that a political statement of the economic situation ran parallel to the moral issue. The triumph of slavery became potentially the triumph of disunion. As the forties merged into the fifties, the two issues, human freedom and political union, became welded into one cause. America, which had become a continental political entity, was stirred by the turmoil of the fifties as Adams and the colonial revolutionists stirred it three-quarters of a century before. The sheer right or wrong of the causes in the fifties, as between the Southern plantation oligarchy and the Northern industrial civilization, cannot be accurately assessed and finally determined any more than the rights of the Tories before 1776 with their friends of the established order and the wrongs of the rebelling colonists can be set down in contrasting black and white in the first cycle of our history. There were wrongs and rights on both sides. Wrong was upheld and right violated a score of times on each side. Sam Adams was no angel in the Boston caucus.

John Brown, another crank and visionary, a ne'er-do-well and failure, had less shadow of legal right at Osawatomie and Harper's Ferry than Sam Adams in ordering British troops out of Boston; but not much less. Though each rebel succeeded, in spite of the legal obliquity which historians may cast upon him, his success shows us what humble instruments God uses for his purposes.

Epochs are not begotten by men in top hats.

Only as the aspirations of common men are stirred by the clamor of other common men, sometimes most unpromising common men, occasionally unwholesome common men, often unbalanced common men, do the great seismic disturbances that separate the eras of history crash into the world. John Locke, sitting by his fire writing his "Essay concerning Human Understanding," expounding in his cloister the theory of the natural rights of man, could not know that his thesis would be translated into human institutions by two disheveled, disgruntled, irresponsible, possibly neurotic protagonists of dissension and disorder who were to release, amid blood and turmoil, the spirit of wicked strife and cruel war. He did not dream what institutions would rise like genii from the smoke of his hearth!

It is curious to observe in any political upheaval how economic issues stated in moral terms attract politicians. Your politician is not given deeply to convictions. He is a creature of self-interest. He requires votes. When he sees moral upheaval in one section of the community, he tries to turn that turmoil to his own political advantage. He creates factions in parties; overturns and demolishes parties; he even makes new parties. And lo! he becomes a patriot, this very ordinary, self-seeking politician; and dies a statesman, perhaps! There comes into every political or spiritual movement a time when its original agitators fall back in all their dishabille and disorder of mind, body, and soul. The neurotics, the cranks, the wild men of new causes give way to your sleek, respectable, stall-fed politicians. So it was after '76 in the Revolution: Adams had begun to fade. Washington was emerging. So it was after '56 in the second cycle of our history. The politicians had thrown their grappling hooks into the cause of freedom and union. Then came Frémont, Lincoln, and Seward; men of class and standing, in high hats and tail coats, who would not look well dragged down the streets of towns by mobs. And they did not come in a hurry to the Abolition cause. We must not forget that when one of the early Republican conventions met at Springfield Lincoln made an urgent engagement out of town. He was not sure of the timeliness of his cause. He was convinced of its moral soundness, but not convinced of its political expediency. Lincoln was only a man; a most human creature, a demigod in kindness rather than in daring. It took the applause of the Lincoln-Douglas debates to enlist Lincoln heart and soul in the anti-slavery cause. At that time it was called the Abolition Cause chiefly by its enemies. Its friends preferred to give it respectability by calling it the Union Cause! In three decades of agitation the Cause became affected by considerable political power. So, defending Unionism, America again drifted into Civil War. And slavery which had been an economic maladjustment, became, through the alchemy of politics and statecraft, an overwhelming political issue for which men gave their blood and treasure.

When the Civil War was ended, a period followed curiously like that ten years between the surrender at Yorktown and the adoption of our Constitution; a period of disturbance, a time of uncertainty, a decade in which thoughtful men wondered whether the war might not have been in vain, whether the price paid for freedom and union was not too high. In that time between '69 and '79 of the nineteenth century, as in the other decade between '79 and '89 of the eighteenth century, incipient rebellions were always brooding. The agitators who had pioneered in the cause of human freedom were bitterly disillusioned. The politicians were in the saddle. The respectables, the competents, and alas! sometimes the unscrupulous, ruled the land. And what the Tories suffered in contumely just before the Revolution, during it, and before the adoption of the Constitution, the Southern oligarchy suffered in reconstruction days. If after war men could only be wise victors, wars would mean something. But in war men learn hate and judgment leaves them. So wars breed madness, and the peace of force brings folly and futility and waste.

It was in these days of the late sixties and the seventies, and, to an extent, far into the eighties, that again in our history came a period of reaction from the futile waste and folly of revolution. The high altruistic vision of the Abolitionists had to go through a change.

Even as the ideals of the pre-revolutionary agitators were reduced to the practical institutions of the Constitution, so the hope and faith of Garrison, Phillips, and the Lovejoys for the black man and the white had, in those days of post-war reaction, to find restatement in workable institutions. Similarly the dreams of the Unionists had to be recast, first into constitutional amendments, then into laws, then into Supreme Court decisions which sometimes overturned the laws, then into customs which overturned amendments, laws, and court decisions—customs that would actually work among men of good will. It was a time of compromise, a time of adjustment; and to millions it must have been a time of disillusion. Reaction is the necessary process in which high thinking is reduced to plain living.

With the resumption of specie-payment and with the withdrawal of federal troops from the South, we may say that the second cycle of our North American Cathay began to close. They were curiously alike, those two movements for the independence of the state and the interdependence of the states. Only the external ideas were different. The pathological history of the two movements is almost identical, and the source of infection of the ideals is a common source for the two social disturbances: the philosophy which maintains the natural rights of man superior to the rights of the state. That philosophy is predicated upon the Christian philosophy which proclaimed the fatherhood of God and the brotherhood of man. In spite of the two wars which were required to establish an approximation of the two ideals, independence and inter-dependence, on this continent, in spite of all the savagery, the cruelty and the injustice of those wars; and alas, in spite of the devastating wickedness that follows enforced peace, these two ideals institutionalized by our constitution and its amendments finally became a part of human progress under what we like to call a Christian civilization. The injustice, the brutalities of war men had to endure because men are created as they are, and will not take truth except through force and at an horrible cost. God speaks the truth through men, through his prophets of philosophy. He whispers truth to men through his children, the humble, the despised and rejected of men. God even tries to tell men truth through the temple Pharisees; men who go down the Damascus road and see a great light. But the human heart is impervious to truth save as it comes through hard and cruel ways, through bitter years and great humiliations. How long, oh Lord, how long—has been the lament of Wisdom to her dumb children through all the ages!

THE LATER AMERICAN CYCLE

CHAPTER IV

THE LATER AMERICAN CYCLE

A most dangerous and incendiary doctrine is this that man has natural rights. If he has one natural right then, by inference, he has many natural rights. Indeed, he has any that he can impose by force. Kings and persons in high places saw this when they read the philosophy of John Locke who proclaimed the natural rights of man in 1700. With pardonable horror they saw him overturning dynasties, overthrowing societies, establishing constitutions which would have to be amended and expanded and re-written, creating new social orders which in turn would be sloughed off for newer social orders, world without end. Sam Adams, "the chief incendiary" of the revolution, proclaimed that it was a natural right of man to be represented in a government which taxed him. That principle was abhorrent to all governments in the eighteenth century. Taxation was a natural right of governments, the prerogative of kings and parliaments which were instituted divinely with full authority over the destiny of the common man. To proclaim his rights as against the prerogatives of the state was treason. But the treason of 1770 became the Declaration of Independence of 1776. Then when our Constitution had set down the limitations of human liberty with proper regard for such compromises as man must make who lives in peace with his neighbor, another group appeared, unimportant people, noisy people, crack-brained people whose logical processes were not restrained by due consideration for the established order. These new agitators began to proclaim a new code of human rights, a code which held the right of man to choose his master. And we had the Abolitionists going at full tilt. The right of man to choose his master being established in constitutional guarantees and the country for a second time having settled down to enjoy the fruits of its liberty, another group appeared even during the uncertain days of our political settlement, even in the reconstruction days of the seventies. These doctrinaires went back to old John Locke, again the philosopher, who proclaimed the natural rights of man. And in the seventies of the nineteenth century we in America had in various disguises the rather startling doctrine that man has a right to enjoy a certain minimum of return for his labor, a certain number of the blessings of civilization which he works to maintain. Now this doctrine was not at first proclaimed so badly as this. A doctrine rarely ever is proclaimed in its lowest terms. Political independence was not proclaimed by Adams and the pre-revolutionary agitators until the revolution was upon them. The indissoluble union of the states was not written in blood as Republican doctrine until the guns boomed at Sumter. But this doctrine that a man has a right to participate considerably in the civilization which his labor maintains is even now carefully covered with political camouflage, disguised in opportunist issues, hidden in all sorts of protestations of individualism. Yet for nearly fifty years in America, this doctrine of a broader right of man has been insinuating itself into American politics. It has been a paramount issue in a half dozen campaigns under various aliases. And the history of this new doctrine is curiously parallel to the history of the two other political precepts which upset politics and business on the American continent in the two centuries preceding this. It was in the early seventies in the very midst of our reconstruction troubles that a contentious group of political malcontents began to complain against what they regarded as the iniquities of our system of currency. We had "the demonetization of silver," "the crime of '73"; and the phrase "the rich are growing richer and the poor poorer" was advertised for the first time considerably in the campaign of 1872. During the decade of the seventies, a minority party most despised and inglorious, called the Greenbackers, appeared. The Greenbackers began making all sorts of charges against the guardians of society. The Greenbackers declared that railroad rates were excessive; that our system of currency prevented the farmer and the laborer from enjoying the full fruits of their toil; that our politics corruptly made it possible for the holders of great wealth to control government and so to manipulate public affairs that the rich would share more than they justly should in the fruits of our civilization. The Greenbackers further contended that laws should be passed which would more equitably distribute the accumulations of our industrial and economic system. It was the rabble speaking, and only a mad minority of that. In those days of the early seventies, while of course there were doubts in the hearts of many who had fought against slavery before the war and in the war, a great majority of the American people believed that the slavery question was settled and with its settlement the world was finished. No other causes of complaint against the perfection of American institutions seemed possible. Any other protest was unreasonable.

So, when suddenly, away out at the left of the straight line of march to the millennium from the contest for human freedom and political union, appeared a group clamoring against injustices that had not been seen before, the saviors of the established order turned angry faces toward the new protestants and poured scorn upon them. The Greenbacker in that day was an outcast. He was denounced as an anarchist and a socialist both; as a traitor and an enemy to American institutions. Contumely and ridicule were his daily portions. He trod the martyr's path amid the cackling ribaldry of an angry people. The Greenbackers carried a few congressional districts, elected an occasional governor, sent a few isolated, bewhiskered faces to the outer portals of the United States Senate to scare the daylights out of the grave and reverend senators. Then the Greenbackers disappeared. The Knights of Labor came with something like the same complaint. They vanished. Then out of a secret society called the Farmers' Alliance, organized sometime in the late eighties, flourishing in the West and South during the campaigns of '90 and '92, emerged the Populists.

The Populists reiterated all the claims and demands that the Greenbackers had so raucously voiced and added to the Greenback mandate to establish a new millineum, a demand for certain political rights as well as demands for a new economic status for the common man. The Australian secret ballot was one of those political demands; the direct primary was another; the initiative and referendum was a third; a corrupt practices act was a fourth. All these ordinances were levellers taking away political privileges from the powerful and entrenching the common man in a stronger political position.

We must pause here a moment to recall that in the 1760's and 70's, the Tories and the King's servants called the Adams group in Boston, protesting against the King's taxes, "the Levelists." It was the indignant complaint of the South that Phillips was levelling the races. The tendency of politics west of Jerusalem for two thousand years has been to wipe out insignia, emoluments, and vested rights that distinguish external men from one another.

In addition to the political demands the Populists asked for a liberal issue of fiat money, for the control of common carriers, for the regulation of trusts and monopolies, for an eight hour day, and for certain safety appliances in industry. These demands were certainly levellers. Each of those demands contained an implication that the common man, the laborer, the farmer, the small business man who lived outside of those circles which wielded political and commercial power, was not getting out of life as much as his industry should have assured to him. The rise of the Greenbackers, the Knights of Labor, the Farmers' Alliance and the Populists bore evidence to the dissatisfaction with his economic status which the average man held in his heart. Apparently he had a deep conviction that political independence as prescribed by the Declaration of 1776, and guaranteed by the new Constitution of 1789, that social freedom and the right to choose one's master as guaranteed by the Emancipation Proclamation, and the constitutional amendments that followed immediately after the Civil War, were not enough to guarantee "life, liberty, and the pursuit of happiness" to the ordinary citizen who had no special privileges under government or special privileges through the accumulation of unusually large units of wealth. Of course this doctrine was not respectable. Of course it was challenged as an evidence of moral delinquency on the part of its advocates. And of course it was destined to be a moral issue when some clever agitator could dramatize it and lift it into a dignified rostrum where he could gain a hearing worthy of his talents. In the eighties and early nineties this cause of Populism was where the revolution was before Adams and where Abolition was before Wendell Phillips.

The times saw rising and falling tides; hardly tides, small but significant waves of protest, much like the ebb and flow of feeling during the early part and the middle of the eighteenth century before the Revolution, exactly like those currents which rose and fell in the eighteen-thirties, forties, and fifties in American politics, moved by the Abolitionists. Those surges of Populism had been appearing in politics for twenty years. Third parties had been organized and disintegrated. No considerable figure had arisen. Many agitators were known for a few years and disappeared. These passing leaders came chiefly from the South and West; though in the earliest stage of the second cycle in our history the East contributed Peter Cooper, the philanthropist of New York, and General Ben Butler of Massachusetts. But leadership followed its constituents and in the seventies and eighties General James B. Weaver, of Iowa, led the Greenbacker. In the South, Colonel Leonidas L. Polk, of North Carolina, led the Farmers' Alliance and the Populists. In the cemetery at Raleigh, North Carolina, stands a neglected and unfinished shaft to Colonel Polk which, like Benjamin Lundy's in Lowell, Illinois, a grateful country forgot to complete. Following Colonel Polk came the humbler folk, Senator Peffer of Kansas, Altgeld of Illinois, a firebrand, and "Pitchfork" Tillman of South Carolina, "Bloody Bridles" Waite of Colorado, and Congressman Jerry Simpson, the Sockless! The advance guards of a mighty host were these scouts and pioneers and sharpshooters of reform—"some in rags and some in tags and some in velvet gowns," but none, alas, destined to wear the laurels of deathless fame.

Fame was not ready to knight the crusader in the Populist cause until 1896. Then entered William Jennings Bryan. He might have been a reincarnation of Wendell Phillips or Sam Adams. He was an orator, as they were; an agitator, as they were; a man of tremendous emotions, in those days of the mid-nineties, as his predecessors had been in the preceding struggles. And he did a mighty work, a work which in the education of a democracy is a highly necessary work if public sentiment organizes, develops a will, and goes into action. It is all very well to say that the Bryan of the mid-nineties was wrong in every remedy for the evils he diagnosed. So was Wendell Phillips. And, so far as that goes, Sam Adams was no seer. All three were agitators: men who stirred the emotions of a populace until its will appeared and so action followed. They were doctors whose prescriptions were bad but whose diagnosis was instinctively right. Sam Adams, Wendell Phillips, and William Jennings Bryan as types have many points in common. Adams was a Harvard graduate; not much of a scholar, a debater. Phillips also was a Harvard graduate; a lawyer from the Cambridge law school. And Bryan also was a college graduate. He came from an Illinois college and studied at a law school in Chicago. The arts and graces of rhetoric which all three had, Adams, Phillips, and Bryan, they practiced in college. No ignorant, back-woods ranters were they but polished debaters, skilled fencers with syllogisms, adept in all the platform arts. Adams wrote; the others spoke. But their methods were the same. Essentially their tasks were identical. Practically their results were the same.

A generation after the event finds it hard to realize the whacking dramatics of Bryan's first nomination for the presidency in 1896. A later generation saw him a heavy-jowled stout old gentleman, bald and with too much hair around the back of his collar, whose smile was a bit too complacent, and whose ways were a shade disingenuous. But in June, 1896, Bryan came up out of Nebraska a young man, barely thirty-six, just old enough constitutionally to qualify as president if he were elected. He had served a term in Congress. He had lectured around the country as a lyceum and Chautauqua favorite. He had composed a set speech. Once he had spoken parts of it in Congress. Several times he had unleashed it before lecture room audiences. He was a college orator and his "delivery" was good. So in the national Democratic convention he was primed. The contention of the occasion was a fight to overthrow the old Democracy of Grover Cleveland and put in the Populist Democracy of the South and West. Cleveland had just finished his second term. He had offended labor by quelling a strike with federal troops sent to Illinois against the will of Governor Altgeld. In the proceedings of the convention there was a lull while a committee was out, and the delegates were listening to speeches of various statesmen. Altgeld had spoken. He was too radical. Tillman had raged impotently—a heathen! Two conservative friends of Cleveland had tried to hold the crowds, and failed, and from the Nebraska delegation and somewhat from over the house came calls for Bryan—the unknown exorciser. He came rather too readily, but eagerly withal, bursting with his message—the set speech of his lyceum nights and Chautauqua days. He stood before the hot angry convention, a straight, lithe youngster, with a fine poll of black hair, and flashing dark eyes, smiling a smile that was to be famous, and then, alas, because time is inexorable, to become fatuous.

Altgeld's tones were raucous; Tillman's voice hysterical; the conservatives too oily. But Bryan's voice was soft, silvery, soothing. He reached every corner of the big hall. And he knew what he was saying and his "delivery" was good. "The boy orator of the Platte" arrived. He presented no arguments. He merely stated the case of the average man, the demand of the farmer and laborer for justice in a civilization which they were helping to make. The speech was electrical with emotion. The issue of the hour was "free silver." He closed with a climactic figure: "You shall not press down upon labor this crown of thorns. You shall not crucify mankind upon the cross of gold." The convention went stark mad. He was nominated for president that day. Like a mushroom his cause burst out of the soil of Populism. Hundreds of thousands of strict party Democrats accepted the doctrine of their presidential leader. Bryan became a national menace. He was defeated only by the organized coöperation of non-partisan conservatism in the North. He appeared again as the presidential nominee of his party in 1900, and while he was defeated in the convention of 1904, he demonstrated that he was the leader of his party that year, and in

1908, he was nominated by his party for the presidency the third time. And he, himself, from the floor of the convention in 1912, named Wilson as the party leader. He was in all those years a dramatic courageous fighter. His judgment was bad; but his strategy in convention was splendid in its daring.

Bryan as a leader was strong only upon his feet. He spoke well, and thought badly. His feeling was sound. His reasoning was negligible. He contributed no thought to his age, yet set masses to feeling the injustice of the age. He was undependable in council, undefeatable in crises—a clarion voice, a noble heart, a clumsy mind. Yet under him the cause of Populism grew until it captured the nation in 1912 with the election of Woodrow Wilson.

Of course Roosevelt came, opposed the emotionalism of Bryan with judgment, formulated the Roosevelt policies, which put into workable ideals the vague complaints of the Populists. Roosevelt saw his policies realized in laws and institutions even if Wilson sponsored those policies at the last. But as Roosevelt policies they will be known. And as the father of the Progressive movement Roosevelt will live in history. So the pathological history of movements is marked by the lives of its leaders. The John the Baptist who preceded Sam Adams left no name. Washington most properly took Adams's fame. Lundy, Phillips, and Lincoln came in regular order. Colonel Polk, Bryan, and Roosevelt composed the triumvirate of Populism. The types ran true. The causes grew after an old fashion. And Adams, Phillips, and Bryan stand out together as three typical rebels; not as isolated men. For they lead groups, they are protagonists of revolution in our American history. And alas! Each of them was a Moses who never entered the promised land. When the Roosevelt monument, a great mountain of bronze and marble, shall be completed upon some hill just out of Washington, three splendid cenotaphs will face one another there—advertising to remote posterity the work of America's three immortal reapers who never sowed, Washington, Lincoln, and Roosevelt. And somewhere out in forgotten graveyards will rest the unhonored bones of Sam Adams, Wendell Phillips and William Jennings Bryan, three sowers who went forth to sow. Of course the reaper who garners the harvest is necessary, and his reward is great, but we should not forget the sowers whose work is just as necessary and whose rewards are meager. They face contumely. They bear heavy burdens. They generally die unhappily. The practical service that William Jennings Bryan did for the cause of Populism was to give it the tremendous respectability of indorsement by one of the major parties of his country.

Covered by various local issues, some of which were sadly fallacious, and some of which survived in laws, Bryan stated the case of the common man in American civilization who feels instinctively and cannot define, his right to a larger participation in the civilization to which his labor and aspiration contributes. Subconsciously the average man feels he is earning what he does not get; vaguely he suspects that many others are getting what they do not earn. The industrial worker, the farmer, the small merchant, fairly generally feel the iniquities of distribution in our American economic system. The principle for which they are aspiring has never been definitely stated. It cannot be stated until it has been examined historically, just as the slavery question as time has answered it could not have been stated by Phillips or even Lincoln in the sixties. It was something more than Emancipation, something more than the Union. Certainly neither Sam Adams nor Washington could have stated historically the principles of the cause for which they dreamed and fought. Probably the basis of the discontent which Bryan voiced is something like this: an opulent civilization in which there is no need of want for anyone must establish a minimum basis of living which shall be guaranteed as a taw-line from which each man may start toward his individual ambition. Certain guarantees of common opportunity in life seem to be in the demand of those who are trying to state in terms of various issues the just needs of a rich civilization thoroughly committed to capitalism as an economic system. For the preachers of the new discontent have no thought of overthrowing capitalism. These needs have been growing for two centuries and we may say roughly that the common man is demanding of society four things:

First, the right to an education for himself and his family; an education which shall fit him to understand and enjoy the complicated life which he works to maintain;

Second, the right to work regularly at a minimum annual wage which

Third, shall permit him to possess as an undisputed heritage, at least not merely the bare necessities but the common creature comforts of the time and place where he works and lives: Wholesome food, a decent dwelling, respectable clothing, access to books and the arts, time and place for play.

Fourth, freedom of opportunity to go forward to whatever destiny his aspiration can push his talents, without finding those who hold special privileges crowding him back.

This share in civilization he demands as a right. It is the newer freedom, the necessary commitment of any freedom in the modern world.

Of course this rather loose statement of the ideals of the common man is not a program, not a platform, yet it underlies most of the liberal programs of the last quarter of a century in American politics. The "Roosevelt policies" put into terms of definite issues most of this vision for justice which lies in the heart of the American people. It is Populism up to 1912. As Roosevelt's influence waned, Wilson's came. And, because Bryan had impregnated the Democratic Party with Populism, and because Roosevelt had split the Republican party over

Populism, Wilson from 1913 to 1917 wrote into the statutes of our country many of these aspirations of an earlier day. Yet they were so obviously Rooseveltian that Wilson had small credit for them. And besides Wilson was stating in terms of peace and on a world stage another and fifth aspiration of the common man: that he shall be relieved of war and its burdens.

No one knows whether the contest of Populism is finished or not. That we have come to a standstill, no one can doubt; possibly the waters are dammed and the current still flows strong behind them; possibly the waters are still waiting for some new current, some new urge in the heart of man, to form new events which shall run the old issue into new channels. These are years of reaction. The reaction is the common consequence of war. It always comes. After the Revolutionary War, the reaction from '79 to '89 meant the birth of a new national spirit. Old issues were realized. New issues were gestated. After the Civil War, in the reactionary years of reconstruction, the political phenomena were not materially different from those after the Revolutionary War. But these wars were fought to settle definite issues over which the people had been quarrelling for half a century and more. Indeed the Revolutionary and the Civil Wars did settle these issues at least so that after each war the dispute could be put into a constitution, or in certain amendments to a constitution. This World War, however, was not fought upon the issues of Populism. It merely stopped the progress of that issue. Perhaps it killed the issue. Certainly in these days there is small evidence of life among those political forces which a decade and a half ago were the militant controlling forces of American politics. Perhaps our third cycle has ended. Perhaps we are about to begin a new cycle. No one may say now.

That we are in a period of reaction today should discourage no one. We are merely trying out our theories. The fact that our theories, many of them, have been stated in terms of statutes is no matter. Statutory dreams must stand the test of practical life. We have no laws of the Medes and Persians. So to-day we are examining carefully in practical living much that we took for granted and made into laws in those days of high adventure, in the first two decades of the century. The good will withstand the reaction of conservatism. The bad will fail, and the sooner it fails the quicker we may go on to newer and better things.

This much, however, is fairly certain. If the cycle of Populism is finished, if its contending forces are indeed at rest, then we shall soon see, perhaps far to the left of the old battle ground, coming evidences of another struggle. And we of this passing generation who fought the old fight, we who were so ready to go out and grapple with whatever dragons of iniquitous injustice the day and times afforded, we shall turn our heads to the place of the new brawl with blind eyes. We shall not understand. To us it will seem a meaningless brawl, a noisy babble of sound and fury, meaning nothing. Each generation fights its own fight, and it is one of Fate's major curses, or perhaps one of the precious blessings of God—as you will—that men rarely are called for the second enlistment. It is of course possible that we are merely living under a few years of reactionary armistice—a truce called by the World War! Possibly the Populist cycle is not completed. Maybe we shall again press forward on the old battle line. If so we must find new leaders. For the old leaders are gone: Roosevelt, Wilson, La Follette, Bryan, each made his exit within the six years following the close of the World War. "All, all are gone, the old familiar faces!" When new leaders come, new recruits will be required; a new army ready to stand again at a new Armageddon. One thing we may know, whether the third cycle is finished or not, whether a new cycle is about to begin or not: these stale, dull days of futile reaction are not blessed days of high adventure. They are days in the winter of some deep discontent from which shall spring, in the mysterious alchemy of God's purpose, the splendid beauty of another spring.

But as we go into the next emprise of progress, let us not put too much reliance upon the arm of politics. Looking over America today, where do we find a statesman of the first order, or even of a decent second order? Yet we are not without our useful men, men who are contributing tremendously to progress. In any list of great Americans today, at least half of them would be men of affairs, inventors, organizers of industry, dreamers in steel and stone and iron. While we have been wrangling for a quarter of a century in politics to give the average man his share of the things of life by law, behold, out of the machines, out of the workshops, out of the great factories where mass production is reducing the cost of a thousand luxuries to the price of comforts, and the price of a million comforts to the still lower price of necessities, the genius of America is distributing the awards of industry with vastly more equity than laws could possibly distribute these rewards. So that out of industry an economic justice of a sort is rising. It is not justice of the highest sort, but it is settling into customs deeply and without legal warrant or compulsion an equitable distribution of the fruits of industry in civilization that is making the dreams of even our modern Utopians rather inadequate. Transportation, communication, food, housing, books, music, all are coming to the home of the common man, the average worker. The backwoods are about to be abolished. We are becoming urban on our farms. Machines are standardizing the American mind and heart. This standardization is somewhat a levelling and has in it much that is dangerous. Yet this standardization externally brings to us those economic equities which were the dreams of the reformers a generation ago. Perhaps our next great crusade will be to reform the dreams that our reformers dreamed; to reconstruct this vast machine-made democracy, living somewhat in economic justice, into a nation of aspiring citizens wherein each individual shall strive to find in the wilderness of standards, God's most unique and precious gift—a man's own soul.

WHAT OF THE FUTURE?

CHAPTER V

WHAT OF THE FUTURE?

If in America we shall ever have pictures of great moments in our politics—turning-points of history—three figures should be put upon canvas to symbolize the birthdays of three revolutions in our national life. First, we should have the tall slovenly figure of Sam Adams, shabbily dressed, coming out of the Boston town meeting in March 1770, crossing the Common, head down like a bull, going to Governor Hutchinson to demand the removal of the royal troops from the city. Then we should see Wendell Phillips in Fanueil Hall in December 1837, supple, handsome, with the Brahmin blood of old New England in his young veins, rising to protest against the murder of Lovejoy, the Abolitionist, by the mob in Alton, Illinois. And finally we should portray young Bryan in Chicago in June 1896, his flashing eyes, his noble head, his stalwart frame, as he stood crying out to the Democratic National convention his impassioned protest against the plutocracy which he saw threatening to overcome his country. Then, balancing these dramatic canvases, we should have the portraits of three other prophets of change—meditative men, but also sowers, who went forth quietly to sow dragons' teeth in the field where the old order flourished. Let us see James Watt in Scotland gazing at the steaming kettle. Let us see Samuel Morse, the artist, watching the electric spark, and observe young Thomas Edison, the telegrapher, making his first magic. For these men were types of the criers in the wilderness who proclaimed a new dispensation in the land.

And all to what end? What is the purpose of civilization? Why is it important that we should consider the results of all that Sam Adams visioned, or Wendell Phillips desired so passionately, or that Bryan's aspiration to justice has implanted in the hearts of the people? What if Watts or Morse or Edison had not lived, or if the things they invented should not have been conceived in the brain of man? What if Washington and Lincoln and Roosevelt or the indomitable captains of industry had not followed to give reality to the shadows which the visionaries saw? What if humanity's leap toward the making of material things and distributing worldly goods had not been achieved? To what goal have we drawn near in these two centuries of democratic activity all over the Christian world, the new world if you will? In what does this Christendom of ours excel the old world, even the ancient world of our own contemporaries, "the yellow, the brown, and the black"?

In the end after all our questionings we must rest our defense of democracy in Western civilization upon its benefits to the common man. Raw as democracy is, blatant as it is, tawdry as it is, democracy does give to the common man the right to aspire to justice in his relation to his fellows. Also he may reasonably assume in his daily contacts a considerable amount of good will among his fellows. This good will establishes credit, enlarges commerce, and widens his circumference of peace as the common man pursues the ordinary vocation of life. But probably we must confess that this security of the average man, in his person and property, does not make for distinction, for beauty, for flashes of genius. In a world made safe for democracy we are levelling men up to high standards of living. But in another order than ours—the old order—the press of vast unprotested cruelties, of hopeless injustices, of accepted brutalities does in some mysterious process crush from human agony, rancor, and terror, the wine of genius. Not in this present phase of democracy will Western civilization produce the beauty and the truth that came out of the ancient East—out of India, out of Greece, out of Judea. Possibly a civilization that exalts man will not grow men. In America during the exceptional expansion of democratic control of life, in government, in commerce, in education, in religion, in all the arts of living, which the last three decades have brought, it would seem that an inexorable grinding force has been at work to squeeze down the stature of leadership in every department of endeavor. Possibly in levelling up the mass we have had to level down the leaders. The cuts may have made the fills. At any rate the half-gods are gone, and the gods do not appear.

How long this status which we boastfully call civilization is due to pause while we develop the forces of democracy further and further, no one can say. But surely one may say that democracy is not an end but a means; not a finality but a phase of life. How many age-long phases human life upon this planet must have passed through. How many more must be ahead of us as we push forward through the darkness toward light—man's long pilgrimage of inextinguishable hope. At times we seem in the past to have made instinctive forward rushes—hegiras to strange lands of promise; from forest to cave, from cave to heated hut, and then to planted field and gathered flock; so from tribe to clan that ventured into the sea and far out upon the broad highways of trade, thence to become the nations of the earth; always moving and resting, and moving again. But surely this pilgrimage of man is not to be stranded forever in modern civilization—even when it is perfected after its kind. When injustice is approximately removed from human relations, surely some higher thing awaits humanity than peace.

Peace for what? Who can say? The race never has seen even one stage ahead upon its journey. Is it not presumable that democracy and its ideals are established to gather men into some vast unity for another flight? Surely these impassioned voices crying across our times for justice, surely all this clanging of machinery, all this hiving in industry, all this organizing of commerce, all this levelling up of democracy, all the aspirations of the prophets of our age for the natural rights of man and the call of brotherhood that have been massing men by millions over the earth with a common mind and a quickening heart, surely these signs and wonders are portents of a new order. Surely we are pipping at the shell of a larger destiny. Well may we cry out with Paracelsus on his death bed:

"Man is not man as yet!"

www.ingramcontent.com/pod-product-compliance
Lightning Source LLC
Chambersburg PA
CBHW030118010526
44116CB00005B/306